Light and Shadow

Praise for the *Light and Shadow* collection

"Thomas Mitchell is a visionary. We are fortunate to have him among us. He is one of those unique beings who can utilize poetry to ground what he knows and sees, a light to guide us."

Lindsay McKenna, *New York Times* Bestselling Author

"Peek into *Light and Shadow* and you will find a brilliantly irreverent, yet satisfyingly elegant commentary on today's madcap world. With his decidedly Scottish poetic style, Mitchell helps us see the absurdity of modern life, the enchanting beauty of nature and the true religion of the Cosmos. This has become my new favorite collection of poetry."

Richard Merrick, Author of *The Venus Blueprint: Uncovering the Ancient Science of Sacred Spaces.*

"*Light and Shadow* is, without a shadow of doubt, the most heartwarming, rib-tickling and inspirational collection of poetry I have ever encountered. I don't doubt for a millisecond that anyone reading these pages of profundity can do so without being forever the better for it. Mitchell's ability to see and describe life with breath-taking clarity is counterpoised by a spiritual dimension that has had my spine tingling from the inner knowing that arises when one is in the embrace of purity and Truth.

If beautifully crafted words bring you sheer joy, you will find Thomas J Mitchell the master wordsmith—the bringer of joy extraordinaire."

John Stuart Reid, Author of *Sound Gives Birth to Light, Conversations with Dolphins and Egyptian Sonics.*

Other books by Thomas J Mitchell

Rosslyn Chapel The Music of the Cubes

The true story of how a 500-year old musical score was decoded in 2006 by Thomas and Stuart Mitchell, revealing a beautiful melody, literally carved in stone.
(Available from Amazon.com and Amazon.co.uk in paperback and Kindle editions.)
More information about Thomas J Mitchell can be found at:
www.tjmitchell.com/

Light and Shadow

Inspirational Poems

by Thomas J Mitchell

AEI/Story Merchant Books
Beverly Hills, CA

Light and Shadow © 2013 Thomas J Mitchell

All rights reserved. This book may not be reproduced in whole or in part without written permission from the publisher; nor may any part of this book be reproduced, stored in a retrieval system or transmitted in any form or by any means electronic, mechanical photocopying, recording or other method without written permission from the publisher.

ISBN: 978-0-9836058-7-4

Published by: Story Merchant Books

www.storymerchant.com

Acknowledgements

Light and Shadow is dedicated to my forbearing family who lent their tolerant ears, put up with my endless observations of Nature, my sometimes wicked sense of humour and, above all else, my extreme eccentricity! A special thank you to my son, Stuart, for creating the cover artwork for *Light and Shadow*.

My sincere thanks also extend to my loyal friend and colleague, John Stuart Reid, for his help and encouragement in making this, my first collection of poetry, available to the wider world.

The Poet

Words indirectly describe
The feelings of the poet,
Resembling a classic Greek vase
Where the words are symbols
On the outer surface,
While a non-verbal timeless meaning
Exists within the inner space,
For which the intervals between
The words create access.
Like all vessels, its surface
Merely defines an inner wordless
Expanse encapsulating its usefulness.
Therefore the poet is primarily
A messenger of God,
Pointing the way to a mysterious
Magical and unfathomable space,
Where the truth exists in the infinite silence,
Which contains and is contained
By the All and Everything.

Introduction

I began writing poetry as a youth during the Second World War—poems that were mainly about my family and almost invariably humorous. Looking back, I sense it was a way of coping with the fears and hardships that the war imposed on me and on all who lived through those challenging years. Poetry became just as important in my life as music; I was taught piano and flugelhorn in the local silver band and as time went on I studied musical harmony. This led me to discover the wonderful link between musical rhythm and prosody—the rhythm of words in poetry—which finally gave birth to this book.

In my youth the famous Scottish poet, Robert Burns, inspired me and for many years I emulated his style and wrote only in the Scottish dialect. While Burns' style has never been equalled, it was fun trying and many of my Scottish-dialect poems have been published in Scottish newspapers. I eventually experimented with modern poetic forms and my writing style now utilizes the natural harmonies present in both music and poetry. I love to explore the crossfertilization that exists between the harmony of spiritual truths and those of wisdom, both of which have grown in me throughout my life. This cannot be achieved by simple prose; the magic occurs when prose poetry conveys what I think of as "the spiritual jolt," expressing moments of greater truth, which, to all intents and purposes, reside above the power of prose alone. Truths imparted in this way tend to remain clear and vibrant in the memory and can be recalled at any time. Thus, poetry can be a carrier wave for those magical moments of realization that resonate in the deepest parts of our psyche, restoring and refreshing the spirit.

For me, the short poem offers an ideal vehicle to encapsulate ideas and concepts that in prose might take a thousand word essay to adequately convey. All poems in this volume can be read in 60 seconds or less, but the messages they contain may take a little time to crystallize in the inner consciousness. My hope is that some of my poetry will create new insights for you when you least expect it; perhaps while driving or going about your daily chores. And for all the lofty thoughts that I attempted to express in some of my cosmic and philosophical offerings, I do hope that my humorous poems bring you back to earth and make you laugh, or at least smile, when you recognize similar people and situations that inspired me to put pen to paper. In short, in this collection I have attempted to provide both light and shadow, to bridge the gap between humor and esoterica, and if some of my poetry amuses and inspires it will have served its purpose.

Thomas Mitchell

Contents

15 Section 1—Humor

16 The Hypochondriac
17 The Middle Class Lady
18 The Magic Curtain
19 Sad Man
20 The Windy Voices
21 A Friday in January
22 The Flaming Saints
23 Doubting Thomas
24 McDairmid's Pets
25 Humor—The Gift
26 Modern Art

27 Section 2—Nature

28 Edinburgh in Winter
29 This Summer's Day
30 On Hearing a Blackbird
31 The Sun
32 The East Wind
33 Snowdrops
34 Mythological Moonlight
37 Autumn Ends
36 The View from
   the Mountain

37 Section 3—Cosmic

38 Our Dreamscape
39 The Golden Thread
40 Dreams
41 Whispers
42 Are We Alone?
43 To Be or Not To Be

45 Section 4—Philosophical

46 Lines on the Death of a Pet Cat
47 Your Brother Man
48 The Dominant Species
49 Our Choice
50 Empty Hands
51 Phantasmagoria
52 The Inner Sanctum
53 Reality in General
54 The Eternal Moment
55 World Wars
56 As Above—So Below
57 When I Look Around
58 The Unified Whole
59 Embracing the Magic
60 The Wellspring
61 Earth's History
62 Considerations of
   Immensity
63 If I could look over God's
   Shoulder
64 The Great Spirit
65 Our Journey

67 Section 5—Esoteric

68 Light and Shadow
69 Evening Thoughts
70 The Allness
71 The Bird of Enlightenment
72 Lest We Perish
73 Who Am I?
74 The Image of God
75 Share Your Dreams
76 The Flow of Truth
77 Rosslyn Chapel
78 Life
79 The Infinite Wellspring
80 The River of Man
81 The Light of Source
83 To Glimpse Infinity

83 Section 6—Extras

83-87 Favorite Quotes & Thoughts

Section 1

Humorous

"The Hypochondriac"—Illustration by Olga Shumailova

The Hypochondriac

She moves around the house slowly
Bristling with aches and pains
Lovingly crafted from the
Family medical dictionary.
After many years of study and practice
She has reached "S"
Thus "serious" infections
Come thick and fast to compete with her
Irritable bowel syndrome, keeping her seated
While the only thing she passes
Is the time of day!
Frustrated Doctors come and go
With reluctant regularity,
While her long suffering carer
And erstwhile husband
Gnaws at the rope on the end of his tether,
Regretting his vow of "in sickness and in health."
Increasingly he finds excuses to leave
The house, longing for the bright lights
And the companionship of kindred spirits.
Meanwhile she sits at home planning
Her next medical crisis,
Which will bring her carer to heel.
Guilt sets in and normality is re-established.
So is the age-old drama of
Love and marriage played out
As she moves irrevocably toward
"Z" and ground zero, at which point
Her carer will spread his wings
And fly off over the cuckoo's nest!

The Middle Class Lady

Her hairdo is unremarkable
But sensible.
Her body is slim to the
Point of being scrawny.
But the waxen face starved of blood
Puts the seal on her
Place in the pecking order.
A mouth set in a wan smile,
An apologetic gesture
But reeking of a patronizing
Sense of superiority.
The eyes do not smile
As the mouth does,
Humorless and accusing
They see the world
As a place occupied
By the ignorant and uncouth.
To an enquiring mind
One might ponder or be
In awe of the manner by which
Procreation might have taken place?
But her forte is her relationship
With the Lord God.
Come the Sabbath she is dressed
Mentally and physically,
To bare her sinless soul to the Lord,
Who has reserved her place
In one of the many middle class
Mansions in Heaven,
Leaving the Earth
To its vulgar hoi polloi.

The Magic Curtain

The curtains on the window
In my bedroom
Show me patterns of
New faces each day.
They peer out at me
From the changing folds
Each time they are opened.
Today an alien with
Large cranium, red eyes
And a tiny mouth,
Spies on us from
Another dimension.
I look again and he is gone,
Ostensibly to report back
On this strange and
Enigmatic planet Earth.
Toy dogs, clowns, sad faces
And Cheshire cats!
All of creation resides
In the inscrutable folds.
And while we exchange
Glances between dimensions,
We never truly meet
Or exchange views.
Yet for those moments,
We have touched the
Magical possibilities
Of other worlds.

Sad Man

That sad man—
Knows so many things
Garnered from others,
Like an intellectual Magpie
Collecting discarded
Thoughts and ideas
From the refuse bins
Of creative minds.
He seeks the fellowship
Of the gifted,
Quoting to each one
A learned hypothesis
That they have already
Assigned to the past.
And thus he sets up
His own academic pawnshop,
Peddling antique intellect
Like the sparkling gems
Of yester year.
Sad fellow—
But annoying nevertheless!

The Windy Voices

The wind got up!
With its many voices
It roared and sung through
Every crack and tiny opening.
It found flutes to play in windows,
Accordions to squeeze in doors,
Each playing from its own hymn sheet.
Then like a medieval choir
Who, having disagreed
Over a difficult score,
Descends into violent cacophony,
As the skills of a conductor seem
To have no place in their orchestra.
The storm finally departs
Over the horizon.
Singing, arguing and howling
Like pub crawling drunkards
Ejected from a hostelry,
Having eventually called time
On the stormy karaoke.

A Friday in January

It was Friday.
The debilitating cold cut my body
Into numerous small fragments,
Each with a differential degree of freezing.
So I hurried to the coffee shop
To defrost mind and body
In the company of an old friend
With a well worn ear!
Old times; new times;
good times; bad times:
All had their five minutes of fame.
Then they were folded carefully away
Once more, in their timeless drawer,
To be revived at a future rendezvous.
Today we enthused about good times
And laughed in retrospect at adversity.
What else can we do, or should we do
With our many years of acquired wisdom,
And our insight regarding
The vanities and silliness of the young,
And the not so young,
Who could use our advice?
Isn't it a good feeling to be
Mature, wise and righteous!

The Flaming Saints

Ablaze with glory
They glare down at us
From an old master's painting,
When Saints in splendor
Ruled the heavenly roost,
Making men guilty for so many
Medieval sins.
Since the old masters ran out of
Lapis lazuli and gold leaf,
The Saints have wandered off
Into the mythical land
Of biblical history.
So where is Gabriel
When we need him?
Where are the flaming Saints?

Doubting Thomas

The worm of righteousness
Wriggles around my conscience,
Stalking me in the dark dank
Corridors of my guilt,
Until it is confronted
By the bird of common sense,
Who swallows it whole
Without question or explanation!
It flies off, filling the sky
With bird-like laughter,
Dispelling any and all doubts
As it ascends into the
High-flung spaces of sanity.
And beneath—
Thomas replaces doubt
With the laughter of
The bird of common sense!

McDairmid's Pets

McDairmid's new venture,
Pet seagulls galore,
When tourists arrive
He's right there on the shore.
"Seagulls for pets, a fiver each,
You'll never find better
On any old beach!"
So they pay to McDairmid
Their hard-earned brass,
Never suspecting anything crass.
McDairmid says, "Thank you,"
Then leaves in his boat,
Counting the cash
The pet venture has brought.
Then a tourist comes forward,
And calls from the shore,
"McDairmid, McDairmid,
I'm shocked to the core.
Where is my seagull—this is not fair."
But McDairmid shouts, "Nonsense!"
"That's your one–up there!"

Humour – The Gift

If there is a God
Who created us,
Then it was He who
Endowed us with
Our sense of humour.
That ultimate bonus
Is the legacy that makes us
More than human!
It observes the mortal traits
Designed to make life unbearable,
Then works its magic
And makes total sense
Of the world!

In the Bible we are confronted
By gloomy Patriarchs
Calling down God's wrath
On a sinful world.
Is it little wonder that
We fear religions
And their fanatics.
But then, in private,
We laugh uncontrollably
At the humorless and
Ridiculous accusers,
And we say to ourselves,
"There is a God after all!"

Modern Art

The artistic Cognoscenti,
Self-appointed of course,
Whose minds
Reflect 'The unmade bed',
Or 'The flickering light
in the empty room',
Walk the razor's edge
Between mediocrity
And insanity,
All of which passes
For modern art.
The inexperienced voyeur
Is trapped by the subterfuge
While the expert Critics
Act it out like any
Costume drama.
Ultimately—
Millions of pounds change hands
And the Cognoscenti
Laugh all the way to the bank,
While the addled voyeurs inquire,
"They must know something we don't?"
Indeed they do!
They know, that they know nothing
About the creation of Modern Art
Except, perhaps, how to make money
From the gullibility of their clients.

Section 2

Nature

The Cobbler—Beinn Artair—
Watercolor by Thomas J Mitchell

Edinburgh in Winter

The winter's night
Grips the City in a cold iron-clad hand.
Footsteps tinkle like ice in a glass
As folks hurry by,
All turned in on themselves.

Their breath writhes around them
In the crystal air
Like a demented wraith
Evicted from tortured lungs.
The sharp cold creeps in
Through every nook and cranny
To nip and paralyze
Like a live thing.

Brittle sounds find no resistance
From the still air,
And, crisp and clear,
The pulses shatter
In a thousand fragments
Against the hard stone walls.

Somewhere, a poor neglected hound
Howls its protest to the sky,
While the moon, presiding over the whole scene,
Shines, with a sharp hard light
And lends its cold white face
To the bitter night.

This Summer's Day

I thank thee Lord this summer's day,
For spreading joy as well you may.
The cooling breeze, Sun's warming ray,
My life fulfils.
I banish thoughts of winter's blast,
And biting chills.

Yet here amidst Dame Nature's greens,
Far distant yet old winter seems.
With waving corn and bubbling stream,
I'll take my rest.
Ne'er giving thought to future time,
For now is best!

So live right now as if your last
And ne'er in future time to cast,
Fearful shadows long time past
Whate're you say.
For now it is a joyous time,
This Lord's bright day!

On Hearing a Blackbird Sing

Sing on thou welcome bird, thy joyful song,
Harbinger of Spring I hearken to thy voice.
By thy sweetest notes our hearts rejoice,
At winter's sure demise, for which I long.

Sing on thou blithesome creature of the air,
Who soaring, meets the strengthening Sun,
Proclaims on high to all, that Life has won,
And asks aught but his song to share.
Sing on thou welcome bird, that song I'll share.

The Sun

I said to the Sun today,
"Surely—
After billions of years
You could get the routine right?
Sunny in the summer
Wet in the winter.
It doesn't take a genius
To work it out."
But then I thought—
Do I take notice
Of the ant's colony
At the bottom of the garden?
At that moment
I realized—
He wasn't listening!

The East Wind

What do you say to the cold
And clammy East wind?
"What do you want of me,
For I have nothing to give,
Especially my life?
You tear it from our bodies
Like a sticky plaster
With your cold surgical fingers."
My body was designed
For warmer climes,
Where the spirit can sink
Deep into the body
Like a feather-down quilt,
And find contentment,
Far from the poisonous
Breath of the East wind
That lies in wait around
The multitude of corners,
Spawned by the high gloomy
Edinburgh tenements, huddling
Together like the bodies they shelter.
If I decide someday to return to earth
I will go where the long cold
Damp fingers of the East wind
Cannot reach me to
Leech my life away!

Snowdrops

Thou pristine flower of lowly station
Yet fills my heart with admiration,
Though bending 'midst the winter's blast,
Thy slender stem and flower holds fast.

And thus on winter's darkened day,
Revealed in Nature's guileless way
Where snowdrops bloom then spring will follow,
With light and life upon the morrow.

Then pristine flower thy lowly station
Yields from the heart my adoration,
That bending with the bitter blast,
Thy slender stem and flower holds fast.

Mythological Moonlight

The moon's cold light
Spills over the low mist,
Saturating it with a pale
White glow, accentuating
The bitter night.
The numbing chill prompts
My body to be aware of its
Mortality, while my spirit
Resonates with the spectral
Beauty of the moon's stage-
Management of the winter's night.
It creates a slow motion light
And shadow display, creeping
Silently across the Earth.
At any moment I expect
The mythological
Venus, Hercules or Mercury to
Emerge from the misty shadows
As the midnight hour is struck.
Such is the power of the moon.
Such is the depth of imagination!

Autumn Ends

The rustling russet carpet
Of discarded leaves
Lies like a cushion,
As if to ease the trauma
Of approaching winter.
The naked trees
Are a stark reminder
As cold north winds
Test the strength
Of trunk and branch.
A pallid winter Sun,
Whose warmth ne'er reaches
O'er the lowest branches,
Does nothing
To disturb their slumber.
With the biting chill of shorter days
Winter's darkness closes in,
And Autumn ends.

The View From The Mountain

In the high places of the mountain,
Above the miasma and
The clamor of human affairs,
The clean clear air
And nature's silence
Is broken only by
The cry of the eagle,
Or the song of the wind
As it reaches up to commune
With the towering peaks.

For the dedicated climber,
It is a spiritual quest,
To conquer the mountain
And thus his own fears.
Reaching upward
To the sacred peaks,
Where dwells the
Spirit of the mountain.

When the view heals his spirit
By his own endeavors,
He is raised above the underworld
Knowing from this moment
That he cannot return
To the vale of sleep.

His view of life is;
Now and always,
The view from the mountain.

Section 3
Cosmic

Whirlpool Galaxy—detail
NASA, ESA, S. Beckwith and the Hubble Heritage Team

Our Dreamscape

Night is a release
From the inevitable changes
That the day brings.
Past, present and future threaten us
With pain and loss as each day
Faithfully reports its disasters.
But night allows us to cocoon ourselves
And sink into the primeval mystery
That is sleep.
We hop, skip and jump
Through the Alice in Wonderland
Dreamscape with no discernment
Of our mortality.
That concept is preserved
In perpetuity by our waking hours.
Each day is numbered carefully
As daylight dawns to remind us.
But oh for our nightly cocoon—
For sleep—
And our wondrous
And infinite dreamscape.

The Golden Thread

In the infinite dimension
Of cause and effect,
Events weave a golden thread
Within the great tapestry
Of all possibilities.
Each of us leaves our strand—
Our indelible stamp
On the unfolding events
Within the infinite flux,
Contributing knowingly
Or unknowingly
To the good or evil,
Carried forward within
Humanity's collective thread.
If we can knowingly
Take responsibility
For the creation of our own strand
As it reaches out into the
Infinite possibilities,
Then we can weave our future strand
With goodwill and unconditional love
For all of life and human kind,
To be contained
Within the collective thread.
Thus, each of us
Can become a catalyst
In the cosmic chemistry
Of Life Eternal.

Dreams

Awakening from a dream
In another place,
A sense of the alien
Clings...
Like the fragrance of pine
From walking in a wood.
The other worldliness,
Lingers...
To haunt my waking hours,
And cast its doubts,
Upon my solid reality.
Is my dream reality
Or reality, my dream?

But then in both realities I am me,
And this alone is real.

Whispers

In Life,
I listen for the whispers.
Those far off voices
That speak
Of other times
And other places,
Of magic and mystery,
That a mundane reality
Smothers and ignores.
They hint at former splendor,
Or murmur softly,
Of a future
Bright with promise
And great purposes
Yet to be achieved.
I listen for the whispers,
And I am transported
To the Infinite
And creative universe
Of the enchanted Spirit.

Are We Alone?

Stars proliferate the sky,
Its height and its depth,
They are as our star,
They burn brightly,
Are born and die,
As all things that are created.
They are endowed with Life
From the infinite and inexpressible
Ocean of Creation.
How is it possible to believe
That man is alone,
When we are sailing this Ocean of Life
With a billion starships,
As we blaze our trail across the sky,
Making a mockery of
Man's vanity,
That we are alone?
How blind, how poignant,
That Man should deny
This universal Life,
This bounteous Creation.

To Be or Not to Be

The Patriarchs' images
With their graveyard faces
Stand guard at the door
Of my conscience,
Keeping alive the myth
That the Lord Jehovah
Is on His throne and that
All is well with the world.
Meanwhile, the world has
Wandered off into the future,
While we stand resolutely still,
In the mythical world of Patriarchs,
Saints in glory
And original sin,
All demanding attention in the
Serious considerations of
Heaven and Hell.
Until I pause and think,
"How boring!"
I hurry off to catch up with
The world before it disappears
Irretrievably into the far future!

Section 4
Philosophical

Raphael's School of Athens, 1509—detail

Lines on the death of a Pet Cat

Wee shattered body, crumpled fur,
You've lived your last dear earthly hour,
To grant more life is beyond my power,
God knows I'd try!
It seem so wrong the like of you,
Should die.

No better friend had I than thee,
Who gave its love abundantly,
It hurts me sore that you should die,
With sudden violence,
And leave the house to lie,
In bitter silence.

I bid you now heartfelt goodbye,
No nearer yet the reasons why
God's creatures live, that they should die,
And leave us sorrow
While life goes on unheeding,
On the morrow.

Your Brother Man

Gently with your Brother Man,
No healing mercy grudge him,
Aye, kindly with your Brother Man,
Should you set out to judge him,
For war and suffering down the years,
Lie scattered far behind him,
So canny with your Brother Man,
No rever'd Saint you'll find him.

Gently with your Brother Man,
Whose life aye ends in sorrow,
Aye, kindly with your Brother Man,
For time, he cannot borrow,
Three score and ten, his earthly span,
Then Heaven's promised portal,
So, canny with your Brother Man,
Remember, he's but mortal.

Gently with your Brother Man,
His path's been dark and long,
Aye, kindly with your Brother Man,
Though he goes oft-times wrong,
His history, stained red with blood,
From many violent clashes,
But, he'll rise again, your Brother Man,
A Phoenix, from the ashes.

The Dominant Species

Is it good sense on the part of Nature
To allow one species to dominate Earth,
Despite the fact that they have little interest
In the Earth's conservation?
We as a species are a consumer society
And we are consuming the Earth!
If one can imagine the Earth as a ship
Sailing on the great ocean of the Cosmos,
Then there will come a time
When our species eats its way
Through the bilges,
And Earth will sink without trace,
Taking us down,
Still gnawing on the keel!

Our Choice

We wear our body like a garment
And fold the Self neatly within it
To deal with our serious inner dialogues.
Each eventful day supplies us
With the script and lines
For our part in the daily drama.

If, however,
We resolve to leave our script
Unopened and our lines unspoken,
How much simpler life would be.
Living with our weightless Self.

After all,
Our dramas would remain frozen in Time
as the Self moves on to
Another new day, bristling with
Potential dramatic outcomes.

Ultimately,
Each day we have a choice
To be responsible or to ignore.
To speak our lines or remain silent.
To be either burdened,
Or to be the weightless Self.

Empty Hands

When all the i's are dotted,
And all the t's are crossed,
When all the battles that we fought,
Are either won or lost,
Then time will close the circle,
As Earth demands her due,
For all we've owned, returned in full,
Then all that's left is You.
Were lessons learned on Life's road,
Did you for freedom stand?
Or will you, at the end arrive
With aught but empty hands?

Phantasmagoria

Where does deductive reasoning
End and intuitive knowing begin?
Is it where dry logic with its
Imperfect mathematical structures
Terminates on the beach of the infinite?
That magical ocean where the
Phantasmagoric creatures of the
Creative imagination proliferate,
And enter our prosaic reality
Through our dreams.

As we awaken again to our
Rational reality,
Those creatures slip away,
Leaving their shadows
To emerge through the
Storytellers,
Reminding us of our mortality
And our immortality!

The Inner Sanctum

I look around at the created world,
From my inner parallel universe,
Sharing the products
Of so many creative minds.
Ancient China had a name for it,
Yin and yang,
The Creator and the created.
That which is created can never
Be more than that with which
It is endowed, arising as it does
From the infinite creative
Wellspring of the spirit,
And abruptly, I see it all,
The impassable chasm between
The Creator and the created
The temporal and the spiritual.
I experience the inexpressible
Awe and wonderment of the
The infinite sentience of the Spirit.
I see creations having boundaries,
Limits and duration in time,
To which I am senior.
From this sacred resurrection
There is no going back
For the spiritual eye once open
Cannot again be closed.
And I enter the inner Sanctum
Of the Spiritual Temple
Filling the empty place.

Reality in General

A friend said,
"Aye, He's got some odd ideas!"
They only appear odd, I thought
Because they do not toe the line
To the great generality that is
Looked upon as reality.
That shared creation of all our
Hopes and dreams, where stability
Is a simple fact that all things are
Labeled, recorded and agreed upon.
Thus we have terra firma,
And above all certainty.
A spade is a spade however boring
That thought may appear.
Anything above and beyond that
Is foolish and may be considered
Dangerous to our fragile certainties.
This may be the reason why
Our artists and virtuosos
Suffer for their art!
Their reality is unique,
While our reality is shared.
Are they "odd" or are we?

The Eternal Moment

To know the self
As a spiritual Source,
Creating all and everything
From the wellspring
Of infinite thought.
To know that
You are senior
To all things created.
Then in that
Eternal moment,
The Holy Grail and
The mystical
Elixir of Life
Is yours to hold
Forever after,
Secure in the knowledge
That it is wrought
By your own hand.
And that this achievement
Is your gift
To the All That IS.

World Wars

We watch the laddies as they daur,
The bonny lads that march tae war,
But mony a hert is sair an' a',
For the bonny lads who march awa.

A smilin' face an' a cheery wave,
Frae mony a toon tae a foreign grave,
An' still we grieve across a nation,
For the bonny lads o' a generation.

But what I ask mysel' in grief,
For King an' country's nae relief?
There has tae be anither wey,
Than asking bonny lads tae die.

An' still we watch them march awa,
A generation new tae war,
A smilin' face, a cheery wave,
An' a bonny lad tae a foreign grave.

Epilogue:
For countless years they've marched and fought,
And hard won victories come to nought,
For King and country, it's power and strife,
But it isn't worth a laddie's life.

With gratitude to Robert Burns

As Above—So Below

As I am poised here,
Suspended between Heaven and Earth,
I see the night sky pierced
By tiny points of light.
I look at Earth
And see the dark miasma
Of human affairs below,
With pinpoint lights illuminating
The collective darkness,
Reflecting the night sky above.
This reflection tells me
That within the miasma,
The Spirit has descended
Upon those unique Beings
Who seek the truth and the magical touch
Of the Universal Spirit,
And from who's caress there is no return
To how things were.
Their light shines within the miasma,
Like the night sky above them,
Reflecting the Universal Truth:
As above—so below,
Telling us that we are not alone,
That the all pervasive
And infinite Spirit is within us,
Awaiting our recognition,
That it may descend upon us,
And that we too may light up the darkness.

When I Look Around

Reality presents me
With its inventory.
Everything is neatly labeled,
Without question or imagination.
Since my indoctrination and
Graduation from Reality College,
A door is a door;
A chair a chair; a table a table;
All classified, tagged and ticketed,
As acceptable rationality requires!

Yet I recall a time
When a door was a portcullis,
And a chair a throne,
The table was round,
Awaiting the splendid Knights,
And I, who knew nothing of
Rationality or labels,
I was King Arthur!

At least for that particular afternoon.
Until the cry went up, "Tea's ready!"
Which for King Arthur meant—
"Game over," as the round table
Was requisitioned for other purposes.

The Unified Whole

Time proceeds eternally
As an immense tapestry,
And in its wake,
Lies the chronicle of events
Into which is inextricably woven
Each Being's life,
Intertwined with a multitude of threads
Which bear witness to their contribution
And the richness of the cloth of Time.
No life moves through Time,
Lest it is a thread within the cosmic record,
Indelibly interlaced into the incredible variety,
Of the warp and woof of Time and Life;
Each Being a disparate part
Of this timeless tapestry,
Reaching for its place in the Unified Whole
And the Infinite Life beyond Time.

Embracing the Magic

As we look around at the world,
We only see the effects of the Magic,
Not the Magic itself.
Hypnotized by its effects,
The Magic escapes us,
Although, we as living witnesses
Are a part of the Greater Magic.
It is omnipresent, multi-dimensional,
Containing all of Creation,
Within the inexpressible ocean of awareness.
The Magic is unseen,
And undetected by the senses,
Yet it is glorified by the magnificence
Of its Universal Creations.
This then is our purpose.
To see with the inner eye
Beyond the senses, and awaken
To embrace the Magic,
And to be embraced by Magic.

The Wellspring

There is a portal through which we enter
The magical dimension of the Spirit.
Each thought, each consideration is created
From this infinite Source,
Which is the bountiful and endless wellspring.
It is that which of itself, is no-thing,
But which, in its operation,
Creates all things.
This wellspring is the portal
To the infinite Universe of Spirit.
You are the Source of the wellspring;
You are the window to infinity.
You are—The Creator.

Earth's History

A rock-strewn peak
And a cliff of
Multicolored layers,
Stripped naked to
Display their ancient demise.
With their colorful lives
behind them they slowly
Weather away,
Crumbling towards
Dusty annihilation.
The violent history
Of the planet is etched
Indelibly in each layer,
Displaying its subtle color
Like the national flag
Of a vanished Empire.
And what of us?
The Johnnie come lately,
Striding uncaring
Upon the solid surface
Of the Earth's history.
Knowing little—and caring less!
While the Earth Mother,
With her long practiced patience,
Contemplates the time
And the place
Of Man's inevitable finale,
To be bonded forever into
Another subtly-shaded layer.

Considerations of Immensity

If, in our imagination,
We hold the Earth
In our hand like a sceptre,
The Solar System
Like a glowing necklace,
The Milky Way
As a shining pashmina
To adorn our shoulders,
And see the universe
From beyond its
Boundaries and its limits,
Then might we hold it in our palm
As a pearl beyond price?
And all this is possible
When we encapsulate Source
To whom vastness and immensity
Are but considerations
Within the creative
And eternal Wellspring
Of the Spirit.

If I Could Look Over God's Shoulder

I would not sit in judgment of other Beings,
I would simply demonstrate to each spiritual particle
The self-evident truth that life is the basic of truths.
I would allow them to sit in judgment of themselves,
For who better to be their judge and jury?
I would resonate with the joy, the love and
The wild and bountiful exhilaration of life, so that
Every spiritual particle that contains those attributes,
No matter how deeply they are buried,
Would resonate in sympathy and rise
In a spontaneous evolution to the joy of living;
To rejuvenate and rehabilitate the love of life
Throughout the Earth.
In this-wise would the purpose of life on this Earth
Be achieved, as it becomes aware of itself through the
Spiritual regeneration and evolution of humankind.
If I could look over God's shoulder, it would be thus.

The Great Spirit
(Chief White Eagle)

Watantanka speaks to us from the stars,
From the winged ones of the skies,
From the creatures of the rivers and oceans,
And from the four-legged ones who walk the Earth.
Across the land His mighty voice reverberates,
And though he speaks to Man, he does not listen.
But in the stillness of the sacred hoop,
His voice can be heard in the silence.
He invites us to listen to the heartbeat of Life,
And from the six directions to find our place
Within the infinite scheme of things,
And to know that we are His creative children.
Therefore, we owe it to our Infinite Creator
To listen to the inner spirit's whispers,
That we may be united once again
Within the Sacred Hoop,
And with Watantanka, the Great Spirit.
Is this not our true purpose here on Earth?

Our Journey

Take my hand
And we will walk through the world together.
As we go, we may gather to ourselves
Other Souls
Travelling the same road.
We will give them our love and support
And show them the way.
Sharing what Life brings,
As that sharing will be our strength.
And when the time comes to part,
That parting cannot break the bonds
Forged on the anvil of Life.
Parting is merely another journey
Which cannot be postponed
And which leads in the end,
To the place of meeting and reunion.
For we, all of us, must in time
Walk the same path,
To a new Life beyond.
It is our destiny to learn to love,
And wait patiently for the love we gave,
To be returned to us in abundance,
When we meet again.

Section 5
Esoteric

Light and Shadow

You can be as a bright light,
Which illuminates the darkness,
Or a dull candle that
Merely emphasizes the shadows.
Ask yourself—
Which would you rather be?
Darkness is simply
The absence of light,
And light defines the darkness
For what it is, that we
Might encompass it with our
Understanding and truth,
Thus to banish darkness
From our lives.

Evening Thoughts

There is a stillness
That belongs to the evening
And the setting sun.
It is broken only by
The hypnotic humming of insects
And the distant bark of a dog.
Nature pauses and breathes deeply,
In harmony with the fulcrum
Of the day's transformation into night.
A golden stream,
Reflecting the waning Sun,
Meanders gently into dusk,
As the departing day
Glides quietly with
A dignified finality
Into infinity....

The Allness

I see the Lapwings furiously
Beating among the
Currents, air driven
Like a thermocline
In a body of water,
Lifting the feathers,
The wings
Over the tree tips,
Sun fed, by beams aplenty.
There, the wing rests the body
And the bee sings
Raucous songs, while
Honey-hunting and flower-foraging
He dances the age-old patterns,
Unknown to the Lapwings;
Each walking the currents
In the great nature mystery,
Known only to the
Mother of all mysteries,
And all is together and apart,
All is seen and invisible,
All is the all-ness
That is the world.

The Bird of Enlightenment

The Bird of Enlightenment,
With its bright plumage,
And propitious eye,
Appears briefly,
Fluttering around the heads
Of they who dream of freedom.
It asks nothing of them,
Except that they follow
Without conditions
To the high places of deliverance.
For those who hesitate,
The moment is lost
And the Bird of Enlightenment
Ascends, soaring to the heights,
Never to return.

Lest We Perish

I weary of man's inhumanity to man,
Of his avarice and vanity,
His selfish blindness
To anything beyond his own
Narrow confines, at which point
The world at large ceases to exist.
Their fellow man is simply
Another opportunity to exploit
For self-aggrandizement.
Would that men of goodwill, who know
Where the centre of the Earth lies,
Might bring light and hope
To a troubled world.
That those weary of the evil,
Can rise and leave the demons of greed,
To journey once more around the
Great orbit of another age,
That they may, in time,
Learn the lessons of humanity
And love for all that lives.
For truly, there is no other way to prevail,
Lest the men of evil perish,
As if they had never existed.

Who am I?

I asked myself, "Who am I?"
The surprising answer was,
"So, ask yourself what you are not!"
This observational reversal
Expanded my viewpoint
To take the universe at large
As my starting point,
And as the universe is the
Almighty's creation,
Which observation accounts
For everything, it only leaves me
My mind and my body.
I am not my body,
It is only borrowed from the Almighty,
Thus it is not me!
This leaves me the mind,
Which is my own particular creation.
I am therefore left with, "awareness of I."
How elegant, how conclusive,
That I have closed the circle at last,
And touched infinity.

The Image of God

It is written:
That God made man in His own image.
Thus, those embryonic attributes
Lie dormant within, awaiting recognition
Of our god-like potential,
That we may grow in spirit,
Within that most delicate state of all,
The Power of God.
This power is driven by love of life
But men have mocked the image,
Creating the evils of war and suppression.
And while God granted men freewill,
It is at one and the same time
A sword of Damocles,
In which it promises
Infinite being or total annihilation,
For such is the power of God's image.
And such is the blindness of those
Who usurp the God-given power of Life.

Share Your Dreams

Share your dreams and purposes
With the light of the setting Sun,
That they may ascend, revivified,
On each bright new day
With the rising Sun.
Thus will your dreams share
The reality and the promise
Of each ensuing day,
As does the Earth,
Rich with Life and purpose.

The Flow of Truth

The harmonic spiritual intention
Quietly encapsulates the
Collective conscious space.
Not as a gesture,
Nor yet as a Holy Command,
But rather as the
Infinite hand of goodwill
And eternal Hope.
Each Being becomes
A terminal for the
Flow of truth and
The energy of spiritual freedom.
Thus is the evil past dissolved
Like morning mist as the
Warming Sun breaks through,
And a brighter age dawns for Man.
Let it be so!

Rosslyn Chapel

As the sun drops gently behind
Rosslyn Chapel,
Casting long shadowy fingers
In the fading light,

Roslin village sinks quietly
Into the anonymity of dusk,
Leaving the Chapel outlined
Against the setting sun.

How often has this evening ritual
Marked the passing of time
As pilgrims sought the mystical truths
Of this sacred and holy place?

Within the walls of the Chapel
Carved in stone,
And embalmed in the harmony
Of its sacred geometry,
Is music and art frozen in stone
For five hundred years,
Awaiting those with eyes to see
And ears to hear;

To peel back the mystic curtain
And bring forth long forgotten secrets,
Knowingly concealed in open sight
From devoted pilgrims for whom the
Ancient truths are artfully distilled.

Life

Awareness is light,
A particular and exceptional
Spiritual glow.
Its breath is Life,
And by its grace
It endows all matter
With existence.
Of itself it is infinite,
And from the eternal
Wellspring within,
Its endowment of Life
Is never ending.
What it is,
Words fail to reach.
Yet this I know—
It is the best of I.

The Infinite Wellspring

In his quest for salvation,
Man, throughout the ages,
Has created a proliferation
Of Gods in whom
He has invested divinity,
And the ability to bestow
Eternal Life.
Being a man-made concept,
It has left the road to
Salvation littered with
The whitened bones of
Failed pilgrimages.
If man can create a God, then
He is senior to his creation.
The truth is to be found
In the infinite and creative
Wellspring of his own
Spiritual Universe within,
Where he is God and all
Is his original creation.

The River of Man

I contemplated the long and
Winding river of human life,
Receding to the horizon
Beyond the mists of time.
What force drives this current
That carries all before it?
What sustains it
When the storm turns to flood,
Or the pitiless sun dries
It to a parched trickle?
It is this great river
That is the genesis of Man,
His alpha, his omega.
The collective Spirit,
Embodied in each droplet, is like a tear
That holds the qualities of joy and sorrow.
But above all it is
The love and wild exhilaration
Of life and livingness,
For such is the power of the river;
While in the dark deep pools of the canyons,
The truth can be found,
For the river embodies its past and its present,
And thus its future.
No part of the river exists without the whole,
Lest it should sink into the dry desert,
To vanish from sight... forever!

The Light of Source

Let the light of Source shine
For no other reason than
You wish it to.
Let it encompass past, present
And future and penetrate to
Every corner that is in your awareness,
Encompassing that which is unknown,
Which you desire to perceive.
Let it be given openly and without favor.
The light of Source knows no barriers.
In its true form it is the Grace of God.
It has no labels, boundaries, limits,
Or duration in time, and all that
You truly are, is within that Source.
It is Life unlimited—give of it freely!

To Glimpse Infinity

To rise above
The corruptible flesh;
To cease to desire
That which the
Earth will reclaim;
To relinquish power
Within the affairs of men
That would blind me
To the pursuit of
My spiritual heritage.
Then let it be so,
That I achieve my purpose
And reclaim
That which the Earth
Cannot take away:
This particle of admiration
For the infinite Spirit,
That I may also leave
To humankind,
That they too,
May glimpse infinity.

Section 6

Extras

Eleazor the Essene – AD 74

Certainly the Soul can do a great deal when imprisoned in the body;
It makes the body its own organ of sense, moving it invisibly
and impelling it in its actions further than mortal nature can reach,
but when freed from the weight that drags it down to earth,
and is hung about it, the Soul returns to its own place.
Then in truth it partakes of a blessed power,
and an utterly unfettered strength remaining as invisible
to the human eye as God Himself.
Not even when it is in the body can it be viewed.
It enters undetected and leaves unseen,
having itself one imperishable nature,
but causing a change in the body,
for whatever the Soul touches lives and blossoms.
Whatever it deserts withers and dies;
Such is the superabundance it has of immortality.

Tao Te King (Extract) – Lao-tze

There is something, which existed
before Heaven and Earth.
Oh, how still it is, and how formless,
standing alone without changing,
reaching everywhere without harm ...
It appears to be everlasting.
Its name I know not.
To designate it, I call it TAO.
How unfathomable is TAO !
All things return to it.
Not visible to sight, not audible to ear,
in its use it is inexhaustable.
TAO produces all things.
Its virtue nourishes them.
Its nature gives them form.
Its force perfects them.
Without a name,
it is the beginning of Heaven and Earth.
With a name,
it is the Mother of all things ...

Truth – Robert Browning

Truth is within ourselves;
It takes no rise from outward things,
what e'er you may believe.
There is an inmost centre in us all
Where truth abides in fullness; and around,
Wall upon wall, the gross flesh hems us in,
This perfect clear perception, which is truth.
A baffling and perverting carnal mesh,
Binds it and makes all error; and to know,
Rather consists in opening out a way,
Whence the imprisoned splendor may escape,
Than in effecting entry for a light
Supposed to be from without.

The Forest of Time – Thomas J Mitchell

Each of us blazes a trail through the forest of time, knowingly or unknowingly. We leave our mark and thus leave the world either marginally better or worse for our passing. Some pass through leaving nothing substantial with which to mark their passing and vanish into obscurity as if they had never existed, and yet, their very existence is a miracle in itself, whether they realized it or not.

I have always known that we must use that miracle of Life and contribute to Creation if only as a gesture of gratitude to whomsoever or whatsoever granted our unique Life to us. If we violate the miracle by leaving without having contributed and having left the world a little better than we found it, then I can see no other way out until that "missing of the mark" is realized and put to rights.

The Light – Thomas J Mitchell

The Spirit is like a drop of water on a leaf,
That absorbs and reflects the light of the sun.
Just as the drop of water reflects the light,
So does the Spirit absorb and reflect
The light of the Infinite.

www.ingramcontent.com/pod-product-compliance
Lightning Source LLC
Chambersburg PA
CBHW071735040426
42446CB00012B/2363